# VOLLEYBALL

# PLAY·THE·GAME

# VOLLEYBALL

George Bulman ·

Ward Lock Limited · London

First published in Great Britain in 1989
by Ward Lock Limited, 8 Clifford Street,
London W1X 1RB, an Egmont Company

Series editor Ian Morrison
Designed by Anita Ruddell
Figure drawings by Jerry Malone
Diagrams by Peter Bull Art

Text set in Helvetica
by Hourds Typographica, Stafford, England
Printed and bound in Great Britain by
Richard Clay Ltd, Bungay, Suffolk

**British Library Cataloguing in Publication Data**
Bulman, George
 Volleyball – (Play the game).
 1. Volleyball – Manuals
 I. Title II. Series
 796. 32'5

ISBN 0-7063-6774-X

# Acknowledgments

The publishers would like to thank the
following people and organizations for
supplying the photographs reproduced in
this book.

DK Abian (page 24); Allsport (pages 2, 9,
36/7, 79 – all by Mike Powell) and BM
Totterdell (pages 43, 56, 68/9, 72, 77).

**Frontispiece: Karch Kiraly shows the ideal
'ready' position to receive the ball.**

# CONTENTS

# FOREWORD

I am delighted to have the opportunity of writing the foreword to this welcome addition to the library of books on the rapidly spreading popularity of Volleyball. Increasingly, as the sport is shown on television, viewers are recognizing Volleyball as a dynamic sport requiring agility and athleticism. This book gives an excellent clarification of the many facets of the sport by including all the relevant information required to play the game.

Volleyball has been described as a game of human chess and the following pages indicate how a very simple concept devised by a Welshman in the United States has grown from being a game for overweight businessmen into one of the big three sports worldwide.

In Britain the game is emerging as a true sport for all, catering for men and women from all walks of life.

The game can be played in sports halls, where the competitive leagues are based, as well as at a recreational level on beaches and grass where it is increasingly being seen and played as a family activity.

The section on the history of the sport provides an interesting setting to the game while the equipment section demonstrates it is not expensive. The rules clinic is a unique section that cleverly answers many of the questions that occur in interpreting rules.

All in all I congratulate the publishers in producing a readable and informative book that is well presented and not over technical. It should prove an invaluable insight to the fascinating sport of Volleyball.

**Richard Callicott,**
*Chairman, English Volleyball Association.*

# HISTORY &
# DEVELOPMENT OF
# VOLLEYBALL

In 1895, at Holyoke YMCA gymnasium in Massachusetts, William G. Morgan, the son of a Welsh immigrant, designed a new game called 'Minonette' in which an inflated basketball bladder was batted by two teams over a rope. The ball had to be played cleanly from one player to another and no catching, holding or throwing was allowed. Morgan wanted a simple game which would be suitable for a variety of physical types, both fit and unfit, and could be played almost anywhere. Morgan regarded basketball as too physical for most people and wanted to invent a new simpler game.

Volleyball's simplicity accounted for its dramatic rise in popularity.

In its early form, minonette required nine players, in three rows of three. Team rotation was a special feature ensuring that all players took turns in all positions on the court during the game. The full playing area was 50ft (15.24m) × 25ft (7.62m) divided by a net (which replaced the rope) at a height of about 6ft 6in (2m).

At the 1896 YMCA Conference the name of this new game was changed to volleyball. Later, the net height was increased to 7ft 6in (2.28m) and the teams were reduced to six players. The court was slightly enlarged and a special lighter, leather ball was introduced. Its size and weight differed very little from the ball used today.

Playing skills developed and it was not long before teams started playing competitively; soon the current mode of play – receive, set, pass, smash – started to evolve.

American troops introduced the sport into western Europe in 1918 after they arrived in France. Before the year was out it was played in England and soon volleyball spread worldwide, mainly through the YMCA movement. It became very popular in Japan and Russia. By then it was seen as a very competitive sport as well as being both an enjoyable pastime and a simple form of recreation.

The first attempt to bring standardized organization into volleyball came in 1936 during the Berlin Olympics. Representatives from 22 countries met to discuss the sport's future at international level and the first international volleyball tournament was at the World University Games in 1939. The war years then gave a boost to the game; many soldiers played volleyball in training, and many used it as a form of exercise and recreation while interned in prison camps.

Before war broke out Poland, France and Czechoslovakia had become the first European nations to establish National Associations. In 1946, when France played Czechoslovakia in Paris in the first post-war international match, the president of the Polish Volleyball Association was also present. This led to tentative talks between the three nations about the formation of a world governing body.

In April 1947 the governing body, the International Volleyball Federation (FIVB), was formed with its headquarters in Paris and with 14 founder members: Belgium, Brazil, Czechoslovakia, Egypt, France, Holland, Hungary, Italy, Poland, Portugal, Romania, Uruguay, United States and Yugoslavia.

The first World Championships for men were held in Prague in 1949, and won by the Soviet Union. The first women's championships were in 1952, and also won by the Soviet Union. Since 1962 the championships have been held every four years.

The Amateur Volleyball Association (AVA) of Great Britain and Northern Ireland was formed in 1955 thanks to the initiative of Olympic hammer-thrower Don Anthony, Roland Harper, secretary of the AAA's coaching committee, and Charles Pegg, national physical education director of the YMCA. Olympic sprinters Ken Box, Sylvia Cheeseman and Roy Sandstrom were all members of the first committee. The first National Festival of Volleyball at the London YMCA was held in 1956 and that same year the AVA was represented by one official observer at the World Championships in Paris.

Volleyball was added to the list of recognized sports by the International Olympic Committee in 1957 and in 1964, thanks largely to the efforts of the host nation Japan, and volleyball made its Olympic bow at Tokyo. The following year the AVA became a member of the British Olympic Association.

Major reorganization saw the four home countries form their own Associations in 1968 and the same year the English Schools Volleyball Association was formed for the development of the game within schools. In 1985 the schools re-merged with the EVA, since when the number of schools playing volleyball has increased dramatically.

At international level the USA are the strongest team in the men's game and the USSR in the women's. The USA men's team won the Olympic gold medal in 1984 and 1988 and the USSR women won the 1988 Olympic gold medal while the men won the silver.

The sport is very popular in Japan where they have 'street leagues'. Business houses also compete in leagues and the larger companies have leagues within their own organization.

The English Volleyball League has been dominated in recent years by teams like Speedwell Rucanor and Mallory in the men's league and by Sale and Ashcombe in the women's league. The men's league is divided into a 1st and 2nd division with five further regionalized feeder leagues. The women's game has a 1st and 2nd division and three regional divisions.

Volleyball can be played almost anywhere. For recreation it does not need to be played on a court, it can be played in a park or on the beach. Many Mediterranean resorts have volleyball nets located on their beaches to allow the sunseeker a break from the tanning process and the chance to engage in a bit of sporting activity by way of a game of volleyball. It is certainly a game that can be enjoyed as a leisure pursuit or as a competitive sport.

**Craig Buck hits over France's world class blocker Philippe Blain.**

# VOLLEYBALL

Today there are approximately 175 member countries in the International Volleyball Federation, and the sport has over 72 million registered players, making it the second of the world's major recreational sports.

*Play the Game: Volleyball* will introduce you to this great game starting with the rules, equipment and terminology. We will then talk you through some of the techniques needed to play the game. We make no pretensions about turning you into an international player. But after learning the basics it is down to you to develop those basic skills. One day you may be an international player, but that will only come with a lot of hard work, practice, dedication, and the will to win. Good luck!

# EQUIPMENT & TERMINOLOGY

**B**efore we take you into the rules of volleyball it is important that you learn about the equipment needed to play the competitive game, and the terminology you will encounter as you read on through this book, and as you play volleyball.

## The court

All volleyball courts are standard in size. The playing surface must be either wooden or a synthetic surface for major events. The FIVB outlaw the playing of the game on surfaces that present a danger to the players, e.g. rough, wet or slippery surfaces such as cement. Volleyball can be played indoors or outdoors, although most major tournaments are played indoors.

The playing surface must be flat, horizontal and uniform. The court measures 18m (60ft) by 9m (30ft) and is surrounded by a free zone of at least 2m (6ft 6in) – at least 3m (10ft) on an open-air court. An indoor court must also have an obstruction-free area of at least 7m (23ft) above the playing surface. In major international competitions the free zone shall be at least 5m (16ft) from the side-lines and 8m (26ft) from the end-lines. The free space shall be at least 12.5m (40ft) above the playing surface.

The laws of the game stipulate that indoor courts must be of one colour, which must be bright and light. Ideally the free zone should be a different colour from the rest of the court (a stipulation in major international competitions).

The court shall be bounded by 5cm (2in) lines which form part of the 18m (60ft) × 9m (30ft) playing area. A centre-line divides the court into two equal halves each measuring 9m (30ft) × 9m (30ft).

Two lines are drawn parallel and 3m (10ft) either side of the centre-line. These are called the attack-lines and the area between them and the centre-line is the front court. The boundary of the attack-lines and front court extend indefinitely beyond the side-lines of the court. The front court is the area in which back-line players may not smash the ball but back court players can do so, to volley, dig or 'recover' the ball.

At the right-hand side of each back-line is a service area which is 3m (10ft) wide. It extends indefinitely beyond the outer edge of the free zone.

Temperature and lighting are important in a game of volleyball. The temperature must not be below 10°C (50°F) and the lighting in the playing hall should be between 500–1500 lux, measured from a height of 1m (3ft) above the playing surface.

Stretched across the centre of the court is a mesh net. It is 1m (3ft) deep and 9.5m (31ft

# VOLLEYBALL

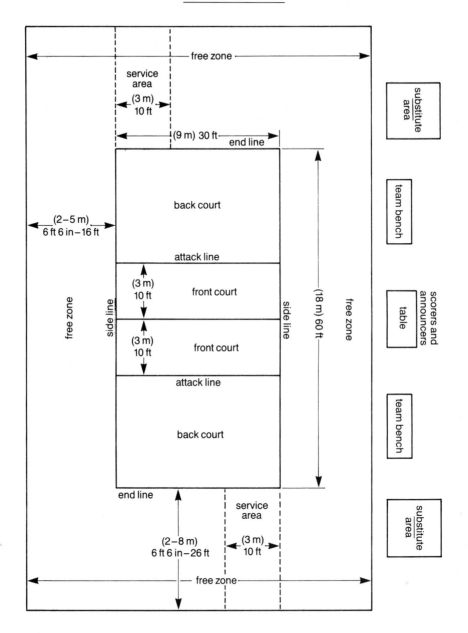

The court should be light colour (e.g. sand-coloured); the free zone dark coloured (e.g. blue or green). The size of the free zone varies according to the status of a competition and, of course, local conditions. The substitutes' warm-up area is at the side of the court.

ball in and out of play

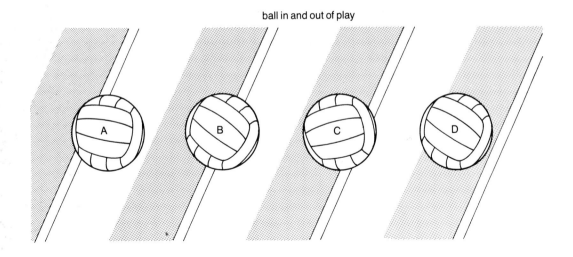

*Balls A, B and C are all in. Ball D is out.*
*(The shaded areas represent the free zone.)*

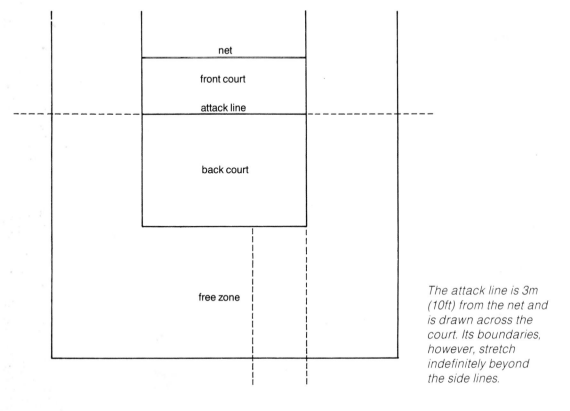

net

front court

attack line

back court

free zone

*The attack line is 3m (10ft) from the net and is drawn across the court. Its boundaries, however, stretch indefinitely beyond the side lines.*

# VOLLEYBALL

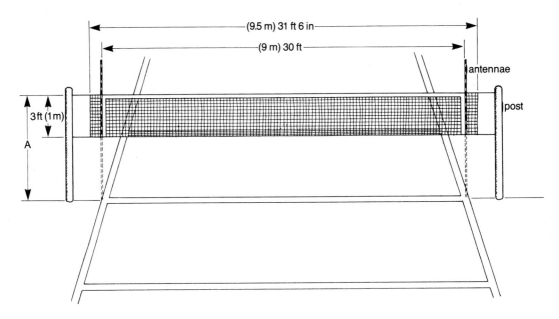

*The net arrangement. A = 2.43m (8ft) for men and 2.24m (7ft 4in) for women.*

6in) long. A flexible cable threaded through a canvas fold at the top of the net helps keep it taut. A cord along the bottom edge keeps the lower part taut.

Two white canvas tapes are fastened to the net at a point above the intersection of the side-line and centre-line. The tape, 5cm (2in) wide and 1m (3ft) long, stretches from the bottom to the top of the net, and forms part of the net. Extending up beyond these white tapes are two antennae. They are flexible poles 10mm ($^2/_5$in) in diameter and 1.8m (6ft) long and extend above the top of the net by 80cm (31in). They form part of the net and mark its side limits. Ideally they should be painted in red and white hoops so they can be clearly seen.

The height from the centre of the playing surface to the top of the net is 2.43m (8ft) for men and 2.24m (7ft 4in) for women. The net should also measure the same height at the points directly above the side-lines as that at the centre.

The net is supported by two posts

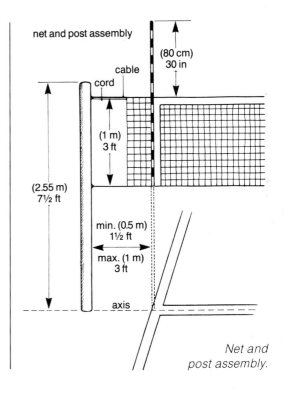

*Net and post assembly.*

(preferably adjustable) each 2.55m (8ft 3in) high. The posts must be between 0.6–1m (1ft 6in–3ft 3in) from the side-lines and *must not* be fixed to the floor by means of wires and cables.

At the side of the court are positioned the scorers' table, the team benches and the substitutes' areas.

Right, that is what volleyball is played on, but what else is required? Apart from six players per side, all you need is a ball.

## The ball

The ball is round, made of flexible leather and with a rubber (or similar) bladder. The colour must be a light one, usually white, and must be uniform. The circumference is 65–67cm ($25\frac{1}{2}$–26in), must weigh between 260–280g (10–$10\frac{1}{2}$oz) and must be inflated to a pressure of 0.40–0.45kg/cm². All balls used in the course of one match must have the same characteristics of circumference, weight and pressure. In major international matches, under the auspices of the FIVB, three balls shall be used.

In a match in which three balls are used then six ball retrievers shall be positioned one at each corner of the free zone and one behind each referee. The object of the ball retrievers is to keep the game flowing by ensuring the serving team has a ball available immediately.

# PLAYERS' · EQUIPMENT

All members of one team must wear uniform clothing (shirts and shorts) of the same colour. Shoes must be light and pliable with rubber or leather soles and no heels. Players' jerseys are numbered, normally 1–12.

In the event of two teams playing in the same colours it is up to the home team to change its strip. In the event of a game being

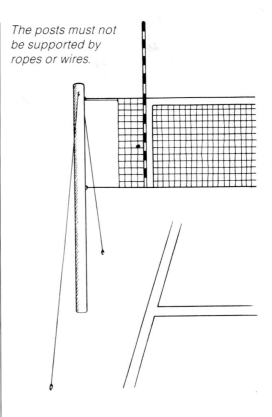

*The posts must not be supported by ropes or wires.*

*The ball.*

circumference 25½–26 in (65–67 cm)

weight 10–10½ oz (260–280 g)

Typical volleyball
clothing.

played at a neutral venue then the first-named team on the scoresheet shall change.

Players must not wear jewellery, pins, bracelets or anything likely to prove dangerous.

## Shoes

It is essential that the sole provides a player with a good grip. It should also be thick because it needs to absorb the constant pounding the legs take when jumping to block and smash. It has been estimated that a player will jump the equivalent of the Empire State Building during a top tournament . . . consequently thick-soled shoes are essential.

## Clothing

It is essential that your shirt is not too tight-fitting, and it should have a raglan sleeve to allow freedom of movement when blocking and smashing. Shirts should be made of cotton and not of an artificial fibre which could burn if you end up on the floor. Shorts should also be loose-fitting. Most volleyball players either have, or will soon develop, strong thighs. So when you buy your first pair of shorts bear this in mind. Ladies tend to play in briefs, like those worn by track athletes, rather than conventional shorts.

Because players are often required to dive to retrieve a ball, you are well advised to wear knee and elbow pads for added protection.

Right, now for some volleyball terms.

# *TERMINOLOGY*

**Ace**   A service that scores a point without the opposition being able to play the ball.

**Aerials**   Another name for the antennae.

**Attack**   The act of smashing the ball into the opponents' court.

**Attacker**   Any player who serves, smashes or blocks the ball into the opponents' court.

**Attacking block**   A block which attempts to put the ball straight down into the attackers' court.

**Attack-line**   A line on the court parallel with the net and 3m (10ft) from it. See also *Front court*.

**Attack system**   The system of attack which a team uses to beat the opponents' block.

**Back court**   The area of the court between the attack-line and the base-line.

**Back-court spike**   A spike by a back-court player.

**Back-set**   A set made over the setter's head to a spiker standing behind him.

**Back-line player**   Any of the three players in positions 1, 6 and 5, i.e. in the back court.

**Block**   The act of jumping in the air and using the hands, arms or upper part of the body to intercept or divert a ball from the opponents' court. A player who makes a block may touch the ball a second successive time without being penalized. That counts as his team's first touch.

**Block cover**   Those players not participating in the block but who cover any ball directed past the block.

# VOLLEYBALL

*The back-set. Player A is setting the ball over her head to player B who will make the smash.*

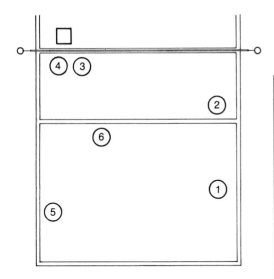

*Block cover. Players in positions 3 and 4 are blocking the smash while the other four players are covering the rest of the court.*

**Dead ball**   A ball that is no longer in play – either after the winning of a point, a side-out, if play is suspended by the referee, or for a time-out.

**Deep set**   A ball which is set or passed well back from the net.

**Defensive player**   Any player in the team not in possession of the ball.

**Dig**   The act of playing the ball below waist-height, with one or two hands.

**Double foul**   When players from opposing sides commit a foul simultaneously.

**Double hit**   When a player touches the ball twice consecutively on the same play (this does not include contacting the ball after blocking). A double hit is a foul.

**Dump**   When the ball is placed over or to the side of the opposing block.

**Fake smash**   When an attacker pretends to smash but then dumps, volleys or sets the ball.

**Floater or float serve**   A service which moves in flight.

**Follow-through**   The completion of the motions of either a smash, a volley or a dig.

**Foot fault**   A server is foot-faulted if one of his feet touches or passes over the back-line while serving. Any other player will have a foot fault called against him if either foot passes the centre-line into the opposing court.

**Formation**   The alignment of players in attack or defence.

**Blocker**   A player who takes part in a block.

**Base-line**   Line parallel to the net and 9m (30ft) from it. The server must serve the ball from behind the base line and within the confines of the *service area*.

**Change of service**   See *Side-out*.

**Combination play**   An attack involving two or more attack players.

**Contacted ball**   A ball that is contacted in any way by a player.

**Court**   The entire playing area, but excluding the *free zone*.

**Cover**   The act of protecting any area of court to which the ball may travel. It is important that back-court players are ready to cover a smash made by their own front-court players, because a rebound often goes to an unguarded part of the court.

**Cross-court attack**   A smash which is hit at a steep angle across court.

# VOLLEYBALL

The double hit. You cannot play the ball again after it has hit any part of your body above waist-height, except after making a block.

Both these serves are foot faults because both feet must be behind the base line when the service is made.

**Foul** Any infringement of the rules of the game is a foul (a list of fouls can be found in the Game Guide on page 30).

**Free zone** The marked area outside the outer perimeter of the court, behind the base line.

**Front court** The area between the attack-line and the net. Front court players only can spike from inside this area.

**Front-line player** Any of the three players in positions 2, 3 and 4.

**Hard block** When the blockers attack a smashed ball.

**Held ball** When the ball is seen to be held before being played. The ball must not be caught or come to rest momentarily on any part of the player's body. If it does then it is a foul 'held ball'.

**Jump set** A set made by a front-court player while he is in the air.

**Kill** A shot which the opposing side are unable to return.

**Lines** Any of the lines which define the volleyball court.

**Lob pass** A ball passed in a high arc.

**Match** A match consists of a pre-determined number of sets. Major international or national league games are over the best of five sets. Other matches (local leagues, etc.) are over the best of three sets.

**Multiple attack** When two or three players take part in an attack.

**Multiple block** When two or three players take part in a block.

# VOLLEYBALL

*A serve that hits the antennae is a fault and is a side-out.*

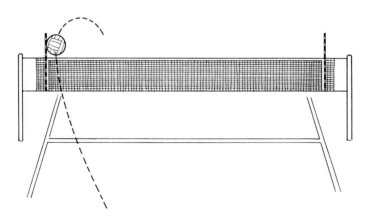

**Multiple contact**   When a player contacts the ball more than once in the same play. This is allowed provided no two contacts are in succession (other than after a block).

**Net ball**   A ball which touches the net (except on the service) is a net ball. If it bounces into the opponents' court then the ball is good.

**Net fault**   If a player touches the net while the ball is in play it is a net fault, unless the fault was caused by the ball forcing the player to make contact with the net or antennae.

**Net serve**   If a service touches the net, antennae or imaginary extension of the antennae, then it is a net service and results in the service being passed to the opposing team.

**Offence**   The act of playing the ball towards and over the net.

**Out of bounds**   The ball is out of bounds (or out) if it bounces outside the court beyond the boundary lines, or the net outside the vertical tapes or antennae.

**Pass**   When the ball is delivered from one player to another without it touching the floor or any obstruction.

**Penetration**   A move by one of the back-court players. After the service he will move to the net to act as a setter thus enabling the three front-court players to each act as a spiker.

**Point**   A point is scored by the serving team and is made when an opponent fails to play a legal serve or return the ball cleanly.

**Positioning**   Players must take up a position according to the team sheet before each service. They must adopt the same positions until there is a change of server on their own team.

**Power smashing**   When a player hits the ball strongly without deception.

**Quick serve**   When the serve is made as soon as possible after the referee has blown for the service to be made. If the receiving team is slow to react it can often result in a point being scored.

*The ball is out of bounds if it touches the net outside the antennae.*

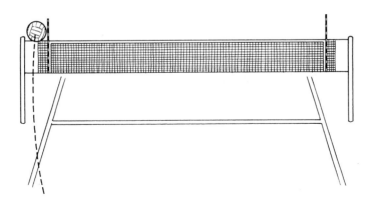

**Quick set**   Used when an accurate first pass is made to the setter. He then provides a short set or volley for the incoming spiker/smasher.

**Quick smash**   A smash from a quick set or direct from the first pass.

**Rally**   Period from the time the ball is served until play stops.

**Recovery**   When a player dives or rolls to successfully pick up a hard-hit or cleverly placed attack shot.

**Rotation**   When a team regains service the team moves round one position clockwise. Only the serving team rotates.

**Roundhouse**   Type of attack shot played with the arm fully extended above the head.

**Scoop**   Lifting the ball into the air with the hands open.

**Screen**   An illegal act by the players of the serving team who prevent the opponents from getting a view of the server.

**Scouting**   Gaining information about your next opponents.

**Server**   Person who serves the ball.

**Service**   The act of putting the ball in play at the beginning of a set or after a dead ball.

**Service area**   The area, behind the base line on the right of the court, from which the server puts the ball in play.

**Set (1)**   A period of play which is concluded when one team reaches 15 points, but with a margin of at least two points. New rules agreed at the Seoul Olympics state that if the score is 16-16, the first team to reach 17 (without a 2 clear point margin) wins the set. Winning scores may therefore be 15-13, 16-14, 17-15, 17-16. Matches consist of either the best of five or best of three sets according to the rules of the competition.

**Set (2)**   A high pass by one player to a team-mate to enable him to play a spike.

**Set pass**   The act of passing the ball to the spiker.

**Short set**   See *Quick set*.

**Side-out**   The change of service. When the serving side fails to score a point by winning the rally then service ends and passes to the opposing team.

**Simultaneous contact**   Contact made at one and the same time by two players.

**Soft block**   When the blockers deliberately allow their hands to 'give' so that the ball is played off them to one of their own players.

**Smash**   See *Spike*.

**Smasher**   See *Spike*.

**Smash-line**   See *Attack-line*.

**Spike**   A powerfully hit shot with the open hand directed into the opponents' half of the court. Front-court players can spike from anywhere on the court. Back-court players must be behind the attack-line when taking off to make a spike (also called a smash).

**Substitution**   The means by which players may be replaced by others once the ball is dead. Six substitutions per side are allowed in each set. A player who has come on as a substitute can be substituted himself during the same set, but *only by the player he replaced in the first instance* (this does not apply in the case of a player leaving the court through injury).

**Switch**   Once the service has been carried out the players can move around the court to take up positions best suited to their play. This is called a switch.

**China's Sun Lisuan demonstrates a low recovery.**

# VOLLEYBALL

**Tactical ball**   Instead of smashing, the attacker deceives the opposing blockers by 'placing' the ball over or to the side of the block.

**Time-out**   A pause during the set when the coach may confer with the players. Two time-outs are allowed per team per set, and each lasts a maximum of 30 seconds. A time-out can only be called when the ball is dead.

**Time differential**   When a player pretends to jump but delays the jump before receiving the set pass. This induces the opposing blocker to jump and thus allows the smasher to smash the ball into the space left when the blocker has jumped too early.

**Volley**   The basic skill of passing the ball forwards or backwards using two hands.

**Warm-up**   Preparatory exercises before a match.

**Windmill service**   A service played with either the open or closed hand and with a wide exaggerated 'windmill-type' movement of the arm.

Hopefully you have digested that lot. If you come across some terms you don't understand as we now take you into the Game Guide, just keep referring to the above Terminology section; you should find your queries answered.

# THE GAME –
# A GUIDE

One of the features of volleyball, and a reason for its popularity, is its simplicity. It is a team game involving six players per side and the object is to volley the ball over the net into the opponents' court using any part of the body above the waist. Each team is allowed three contacts with the ball to get it over the net. Points are scored only by the serving team, and points are gained if the opposing side fails to return the ball over the net, or a winning shot is played whereby the ball lands in the opponents' court. In the deciding set the rally point system operates.

The length of the game varies. There is certainly no time limit on a game, but the number of sets dictates its length. Major international games, national league and cup matches are played over the best of five sets, while other local league games are generally the best of three. To win a set one team must reach 15 points but must have a two-point margin over the other team. In other words, once the score gets to 14-all, play continues until 16-14, 17-15. Should the score reach 16-16 a new rule comes into play. The first team to reach 17 (without a 2 clear point margin) wins the set. There is a break of up to three minutes between sets, while teams change ends. If both teams are ready to start before this, the next set may begin earlier. Coaches can call two

30-second (maximum) time-outs in each set. Players can be called to the side of the court for instruction.

That's about it, what could be simpler?

Understandably, there are further rules and regulations which must be adhered to and we will now outline these. Rules that need any further clarification will be covered in the Rules Clinic on pages 34–41.

## The team

A team consists of 12 players numbered 1-12, but only six may be on court at any one time. The players who commence the game should have their name and number given to the referee by the coach. These players are the starting players and may not leave the court without the referee's permission. The other six players are the substitutes and may sit with the coach on the benches provided at the side of the court or warm-up in the substitutes' warm-up area at the side of the court.

Each team must have an appointed captain. His role, apart from ensuring the conduct and discipline of his players on the court, is to act as a liaison between his players and the officials. He is the only one allowed to converse with the referee over points of law. He is also the only person allowed to ask the referee to check the net, ball or any other playing conditions if he feels they are not right.

Obviously, your captain must be conversant with the laws of the game, and must also be able to approach referees in a polite manner and without getting 'hot-headed', even if he feels the referee's decision is wrong.

It is important that all team members, either on or off the court, play the game in the proper spirit. Unsportsmanlike conduct will not be tolerated, and all refereeing decisions must be accepted.

## Formations

Order of play is decided by the toss of a coin; this ceremony involves the referee and the two team captains. The winning captain chooses either the right to serve first, or has the choice of court.

Players must then line up in accordance with the starting line-up handed to the referee. The team, line-ups and position of players is very important because the **rotation of players** forms a crucial part of volleyball.

At the time the ball is hit by the server, all other players must stand within the confines of their own court and in two lines of three players. The players do not have to stand in a straight line but must be seen to have formed two distinct lines.

The three players closest to the net are the front-line players and take up positions 4 (left), 3 (centre) and 2 (right). These are not necessarily the players' shirt numbers, but the positions they occupy. The other three players are the back-line players and are numbered 5 (left), 6 (centre) and 1 (right). Each back-line player must be further from the net than his corresponding front-line player.

Players of both sides retain these positions at each service until a side-out. When the service changes to the next team then it is **that team only** which rotates its players one place in a clockwise direction.

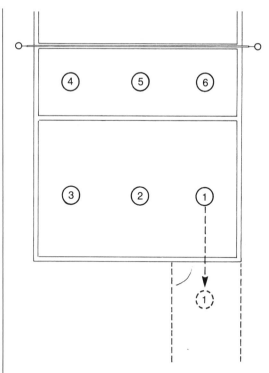

These are the positions of the six players (they are not the players' numbers as they appear on their shirts). Numbers 2, 3 and 4 are front court players; numbers 5, 6 and 1 are back court players. If the team is serving then the player at position 1 becomes the server.

The team which lost the service **does not rotate**. You can therefore see that all players take it in turn to serve.

The rotation order, as recorded on the scoresheet at the beginning of the set, must be maintained throughout that set. It can only be changed at the start of a new set.

Once the ball has been served the players are at liberty to move around the court and take up any position they desire.

A different rotation order can be used for each new set and players on the substitutes' bench can be introduced into the game.

Up to six substitutes may be used per set. Any player who joins the game during a set

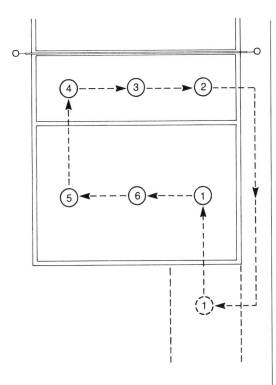

*After a side-out the players of the 'new' serving team rotate one place in a clockwise direction. The player from position 2 becomes the server. Once he loses serve he takes up position 1 on the court.*

as a substitute can himself be substituted **but only by the player he replaced in the first instance**. Substitutions must be made during a break in play and with the approval of the referee.

## The serve

The serve is carried out by the back right-hand player (in position 1) who must play the ball with one hand (either open or closed) or any part of the arm over the net between the antennae and into the opposing court. This commences play and starts any rally.

The team with the right to serve first does so at the commencement of sets 1 and 3. The opposing team serves at the start of all other sets. In a five-set game teams will toss up to decide which team will serve and which team will have the choice of end.

Once the serve changes then, after rotation, the player who was in position 2 of the receiving team (right forward) becomes the server.

The server must be within the confines of the service area but may move around freely and jump to make the serve. Provided his foot (feet) do not touch the end-line or the free zone outside the service area at the moment he makes contact with the ball, the serve is good. He may land inside the court or outside the service area after making the serve.

Once the referee has whistled for the service to commence, the server has five seconds in which to hit the ball.

To make a clean service the ball must be thrown with either one hand or both hands into the air and then cleanly hit with one hand or any part of the arm.

Players of the serving team must **not** screen the server. In other words they must allow the non-receiving team a clear view of the server and the flight of the ball.

## Ball contacts

Each team is allowed three contacts with the ball to get it over the net. It must pass over the net on the third contact or it is a point lost or side-out.

However, front-line players may jump to block a smash from an opposing player. If the ball remains in the blocker's court then the block does **not** count as the first contact for that team. Every time the ball is passed from one player to another it is one contact, or every time the ball hits a player it is deemed to be one contact. No player can touch the ball twice consecutively (other than after a block) but he may touch it twice in any one play.

# VOLLEYBALL

*The three contacts. Player A retrieves after a smash or serve. Player B sets to player C who makes the smash.*

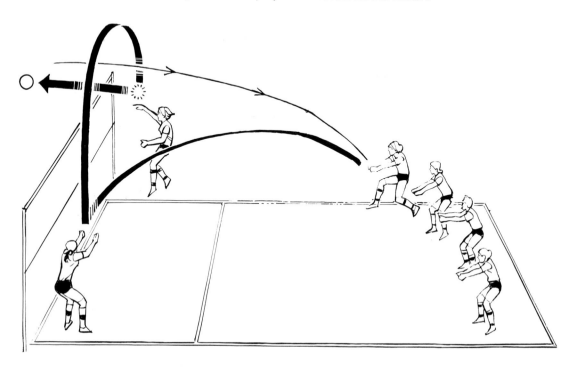

The ball must not come to a momentary rest on the player. If it does, a fault is called for a held ball.

Front-line players may make an attack hit (spike or smash) from anywhere within their own court. Back-line players must ensure that their feet neither touch nor pass the attack-line at the time of take-off when making a spike. However, they may play an attacking shot into the opponents' court from within the front court, but only if the ball is below the horizontal plane of the top of the net.

## Faults

Common causes of faults, which result in loss of service (side-out) or a point to the opposing team, are as follows:

(**a**) ball touches the ground.

(**b**) ball touches a player below the waist; ILLEGAL CONTACT.

(**c**) ball does not cross the top of the net between the antennae.

(**d**) ball crosses centre-line under the net.

(**e**) ball hits the antennae or its imaginary extension.

(**f**) ball is played more than three times in succession by one team; FOUR CONTACTS.

(**g**) two opponents hold the ball simultaneously over the net; DOUBLE FAULT.

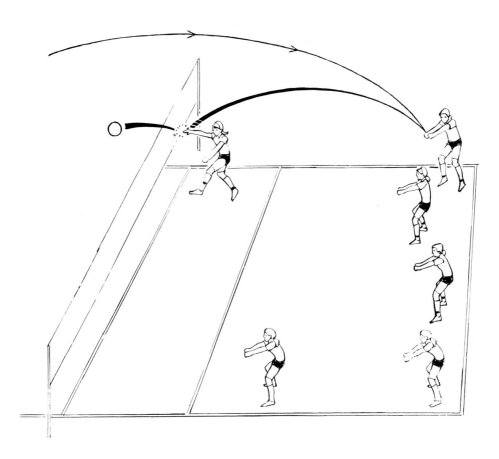

(**h**) ball is held or comes to a momentary rest; HELD BALL.

(**i**) ball is played twice consecutively by one player; DOUBLE CONTACT.

(**j**) ball lands outside the boundary lines, or touches a player or foreign object outside the court, without first touching an opponent; BALL OUT.

(**k**) a player touches the net or antennae.

(**l**) a player deliberately touches an opponent.

(**m**) ball touches team-mate from service.

(**n**) ball touches net or antennae (or extension) or fails to pass through the area, from the service.

(**o**) players carry out an individual or team screen at the service.

(**p**) positional fault.

*You don't have to use all three touches before returning the ball.*

(**q**) rotational fault.

(**r**) illegal substitution.

(**s**) delayed substitution after second time-out.

(**t**) interfering with the ball while in the opponents' half of the court.

(**u**) player entering the opponents' court.

# VOLLEYBALL

*The officials' positions. If there are four linesmen, the other two should be positioned at the vacant corners.*

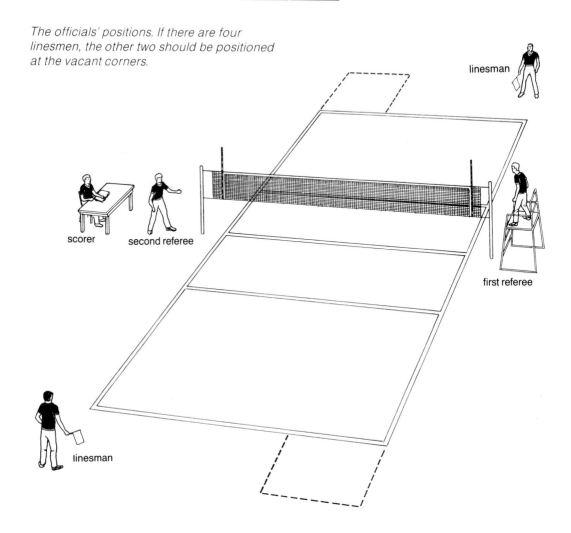

(**v**) player leaves the court without the referee's permission.

(**w**) player makes an attack hit while ball is in the opponents' court.

(**x**) back-line player makes spike from inside the front court.

(**y**) blocking outside the antennae.

(**z**) blocking a service.

(**aa**) blocking by a back-line player.

(**bb**) player receives a misconduct penalty.

The above are faults in accordance with the rules of the game. You will also be penalized for any level of misconduct. Then you will be warned about your behaviour. But in cases of aggression shown towards an official or other player you will be dismissed from the match without warning. The message is simple. Do not argue with the officials and play the game in the proper spirit. That way you will gain hours of enjoyment from volleyball.

Talking of discipline, that brings us finally to the officials.

## The officials

The game is controlled by two referees, the first referee and second referee. The **first referee** has overall control over the game and is positioned in an elevated position in line with the net. He has a clear view of all the action. The **second referee** is positioned opposite the first referee, and close to the scorer's table and substitutes' benches.

Ideally, four **linesmen** should assist the referee and be situated at each corner of the court. They should indicate whether a ball is in or out of court, and whether the ball has been contacted by a player. Each linesman uses a flag to attract the referee's attention. If it is not possible to get four linesmen, say for a local club match, then two will suffice, at diagonally opposite corners to each other.

The **scorer** is positioned at a table on the opposite side of the court to the first referee.

The scorer is responsible for entering the names and numbers of the players and the name of the team coach before the commencement of each game. The scorer not only keeps a note of points scored, but also keeps track of time-outs called and substitutions made, and also checks that the correct rotation order is maintained.

The rules of all games are open to interpretation and that is where common sense prevails. But there are always technicalities, and the Rules Clinic on pages 34–41 will clarify additional points not already covered on the previous pages.

The one thing you must remember: volleyball is a simple game. You may not think so after reading the foregoing pages, but get out on that court with some mates and you will soon realize how enjoyable, and simple, it really is.

# RULES
# CLINIC

**You said earlier that at the starting line-up the players form into two lines of three, but do not have to be in a straight line. Would it be possible for them to line up virtually in one continuous line but with the back-line players a fraction behind the front-line players?**

Yes, but what good would that do? They need to protect and cover as much of the court as possible. That would not be achieved by lining up this way. The rules stipulate that at least part of one foot of each front-line player must be nearer the net than his corresponding back-line player. And at least part of the foot of each right or left player (front or back) must be closer to the side-line than the centre player of the same line.

**Can any player in the team receive service?**

Yes. Service can be made to any part of your opponents' court.

**How many times can one player serve?**

A player continues to serve until his team loses service. In theory one player could serve for all 15 points.

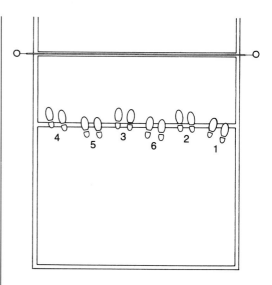

*This line-up is perfectly legal. But what good would it do? A serve over the top of the six players would be a winner!*

**If a player serves out of order, what happens?**

If a player serves out of rotation order his team loses all the points scored by that player on that serving sequence. The team also lose possession of the ball. The team must then revert to its correct rotation order before service recommences.

## What is a double touch?

A double touch is when a player contacts the ball twice in succession. This is illegal, and the player is penalized with the loss of a point or service.

## Can service be received with a volley?

Yes. If in the opinion of the referee the receiving player has played the ball cleanly without 'holding' the ball then the player may volley the ball back over the net. This would only happen in reply to a 'soft' service.

## What happens if the ball hits the net in the course of a rally?

Except for a service, if the ball hits the net it is still in play.

## If a served ball hits the net is the server allowed a second service?

No. If the service hits the net, antennae, the ceiling or any hanging object, e.g. lights, then the server's team loses possession of the ball.

## If the server throws the ball up and then fails to hit it, is this a fault?

No. The player can allow the ball to hit the floor again and then restart the sequence by tossing the ball up before serving.

## Can a match continue if a team has fewer than six players on court?

No. The match is awarded to the opponents.

## Can any player in the team 'set' the ball for a team-mate to make a smash?

Yes, except for the player who last contacted the ball.

## Can any player smash the ball?

Only front-line players can smash the ball from the front court. Back-line players may only smash from behind the attack-line.

## Why must players start each rally in specific positions?

This is to ensure that each player has the opportunity to play each position, both front-line and back-line. If this did not happen the front-line players would all be very tall and the back-line players smaller and quicker.

## Can any ball be blocked?

No. The service cannot be blocked, nor can a 'set' be blocked.

## If a team is found to be out of correct rotation order, what happens?

The referee checks the rotation order submitted by the coach at the beginning of the set, and ensures the players take up their correct positions. If the team is serving it will lose service and also any points scored in that sequence of serves.

USSR's Vladimir Chouriking beats the
formidable USA trio of Partie (5), Ctvrtlik (4)
and Timmons (6).

# VOLLEYBALL

Although these balls are out of court they are still good as they have not touched the ground and as long as they have been played by a team-mate.

*Your feet do not have to be on the ground when serving. If one or both are on the ground then they must not go outside the service area.*

### If the defending team blocks the ball and it rebounds outside the court but is still in the air, is it out of play?

No, provided it does not touch the ground. Once the ball has been blocked the team still has three touches to return the ball back over the net. If the ball is retrieved, rather than blocked, and travels out of court the defending team have two touches to return the ball back over the net.

### Do I have to be within the court area before making a shot?

No. You can be off-court making a retrieve. You cannot, however, cross into your opponents' court to retrieve the ball.

### What happens if, after smashing the ball, I make contact with the net?

If the ball has already hit the floor it is 'dead' and there is no fault. But if it is still in play, it is a fault and your team will either lose a point or the service.

### Must my feet be on the ground when serving?

No. The server may jump in the air to serve the ball.

### If the score reaches 15-14 is that the end of the set?

No. Play continues to 16-14, 17-15 or 17-16. If the score reaches 16-16 the first team to reach 17 points wins the set.

### If a game goes to the deciding set of a match, do teams change ends half-way through it?

Yes, they change when one team reaches eight points. The change must be made without delay and without coaching. The player who served last before the change continues serving.

### You said that once the serve has been made players can move around the court freely. Does this therefore mean a back-line player can become a front-line player?

No. He can play anywhere in the court including the front court, but must observe the restrictions placed on him. He is still a back-line player even though he may be standing in the front court. Consequently he cannot spike from inside the attack line, nor can he block.

# VOLLEYBALL

### When can a substitution be made?

It can be made when the ball is dead. It must be done quickly so that the flow of play is not interrupted.

### How many substitutions can take place at any one time?

Any number of substitutions can take place, up to a maximum of six. A substitute may enter the game only once per set in place of a player in the starting line-up. He can only be replaced by the same player.

### Can substitutes shout encouragement and instructions to team-mates already on the court?

Encouragement, yes; instructions, no.

### What happens if a player's feet cross the centre line?

If the foot remains in contact with the line, there is no fault. But if the foot is clearly in the opponents' court then it is a fault.

### What is the purpose of the antennae?

The antennae are there to ensure that the attack does not have too great an advantage over the defence. Hence all balls must be hit across the net between the antennae and without touching them. This reduces the 'width' of the attack. If there was no antennae the attack would be able to hit along too wide a front making it impossible to block.

### Can players query a referee's decision?

No. Only the captain may speak with the referee and this *must be* in a respectful manner.

### What is the role of the coach at a match?

The coach is responsible for providing the referee with the names and numbers of the players. Before each set he must also give the referee the players' rotation order.

### When is the ball 'in'?

The ball is in when it touches the floor of the playing court, including the boundary line.

### When is the ball 'in play'?

Play starts with the referee's whistle. The ball is said to be 'in play' from the service hit.

### When is the ball 'out of play'?

Play ends when the referee blows his whistle. If the whistle is blown for a fault made in play then the ball is 'out of play' at the moment the fault is committed.

### Can the ball be played by any part of my body?

No. The ball must be played by or touch a part of your body above and including the waist.

### What happens if two opposing players commit faults simultaneously?

They cancel each other out and a replay is called.

### How many players can take part in a block?

Only the front-court players may take part in a block. Hence a block can comprise one, two or three players.

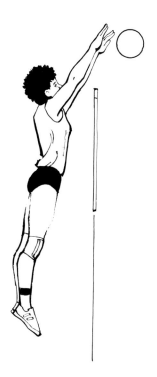

*Hands over the net . . . perfectly legal, but don't touch the net.*

### Can I reach over the net?

Yes, you can reach over the net to block the ball, provided you do not interfere with the opponent's play. Also, if you are a spiker you may follow-through with the hand beyond the net after the attack provided the initial contact was made on your own side of the net.

### What happens if an injury occurs in the course of play?

Should an accident occur while the ball is in play, then play is halted immediately and the rally is replayed.

### When serving, can I throw the ball into the air, allow it to bounce, and then perform the service?

No, it must be thrown and then hit before hitting the ground.

### What happens if two players make contact with the ball at the same time?

This is called simultaneous contact. If simultaneous contact is by opposing players and the ball remains in play then the receiving team shall be allowed three more contacts. However, if the ball goes out of play then the team on the opposite side will be deemed to have played a fault; BALL OUT.

### Can I hold a team-mate in order to stop him committing a fault like running into the net or into the opponent's court?

Yes.

### Similarly, can I run into a team-mate in order to make contact with the ball?

Yes.

### If the ball hits my chest and I then play it with my hand is this alright?

No, it is a double hit.

### If a smash goes into the net is it automatically a point or side-out to the opposing team?

No, a ball played into the net can be recovered, provided your side still have a play left. If the shot into the net was the third contact then it is a fault. If it was only the second, or even first contact, then play can continue until the remaining contacts are completed.

# TECHNIQUE

To play volleyball you need to be able to perform the following five functions: (a) serve, (b) pass, (c) set, (d) smash or spike, (e) block.

We will look at the role of each individually and teach you some of the techniques you will need to master in order to help you with your game.

Classic volleyball is three-touch volleyball;
1 receive and pass
2 set
3 smash

After serving, a player from the opposing team 'absorbs' the serve and passes the ball to the team's main passer, known as the **setter**. He is positioned near the net and he sets the ball up for a **smasher** to complete the attack by approaching, jumping high and smashing the ball down into the opposing court. The defending team have to prevent such an action and they will do that by either blocking at the net or by recovering the ball and then engaging in their own three-touch play.

We will now take a closer look at all five disciplines.

## SERVING

When serving you must remember the following:
(**a**) the ball must be tossed into the air and hit with any part of the hand, fist or arm.
(**b**) the ball must not touch the net or antennae.

(**c**) the ball must land in the opposing court, or on the lines surrounding the court.
(**d**) the ball can be served to any part of the opponents' court.
(**e**) unlike lawn tennis you have only one chance to make a good service.

There are several different ways of serving. All are effective and you are well advised to practise all of them, but you will no doubt find one that suits your style better than the others. The more different types of serve you can master, the better the chance of confusing your opponents.

Irrespective of which serve you use it is essential that you can control and place the ball into the part of your opponents' court that you want. By placing each service you can attack the opposition by aiming for weak points in a team's line-up. But that is where a good coach comes in; he will make sure that his players are so positioned in the initial line-up that there will be no weaknesses after a rotation.

Always try to attack the opposition with your serve, and vary the depth and speed of the ball. It is worth picking out a player to serve to. You may decide to serve to a substitute, adopting the theory that if he was as good as the other players he would have been in the starting line-up. It is always worth directing a serve at the opposing setter or smasher thus slowing down their attacking

**Tomas Hoszek of Sweden shows why he is one of the best jump servers in the world.**

# VOLLEYBALL

move because you have taken one of their key players out of their attack by having to play the initial pass.

Serving is the only volleyball skill over which you have full control. Before serving take your time (within the five-second rule), concentrate, make sure your feet are within the service area, and look at the opposition. Don't forget, serving is a means of getting the opposing team to play the ball. Try and make that as difficult as possible for them.

After serving don't stand in your service area and think that you have performed your duty. You haven't. Get into the game straight away.

We will now look at the three main serves; Underhand, Tennis, and Windmill.

The first serve we look at is the **underhand** serve. It is the most elementary of all serves and the one you should learn to master first of all. You will find the ball easier to control with the underhand serve, but you will not be able to get the same amount of power into the serve.

To play the underhand serve keep the hand closed. Throw the ball from the non-serving hand and bring the serving hand from behind your back to make contact with the ball in front of you at approximately waist-height. Hit the ball with either the clenched fist or wrist. After making contact with the ball it is important to follow-through with the arm.

The legs also play an important role in the service. Keep your feet apart for good balance, and keep your knees bent.

# TECHNIQUE

The simple underhand serve, like all serves, can be varied by imparting spin on the ball by bringing the serving hand across the ball at the moment of contact. A spinning ball is harder for the opposing players to control.

The **tennis** serve is, as its name implies, an overhead serve similar to the serving action in a game of tennis.

This service can be made from either a standing-still position or by stepping into the serve to provide more power. If you do 'step' into the serve, make sure your foot is not outside the service area at the moment of contact.

Ensure your body is square and facing the net. Have your feet shoulder-width apart and, if you serve with your right hand, have your left leg forward. Throw the ball up vertically about 1–1.5m (3–4$\frac{1}{2}$ft) above your head. Your serving hand should be poised ready to hit the ball.

The ball is hit with the open hand and with the arm completely straight, this will help to keep the trajectory of the ball as flat as possible. Keep the arm straight as you follow-through. Your momentum will carry you forward and onto the court and into play. The whole serving action must be in one continuous movement. Don't forget, get into the game as quickly as you can.

The jump or smash service is another overhead service that is becoming increasingly popular, mostly with male players but also used by some women players.

*The simple underarm serve.*
*(a) Concentrate, pick out the spot you want to serve to. Keep your eye on the ball and throw it up (b), then strike the ball with your other hand (c).*

# VOLLEYBALL

*The tennis serve, so called because the action resembles the service in lawn tennis. It is important to keep your eye on the ball throughout the delivery.*

The ball is thrown up into the air and forward so that the player can run forward, jump to hit the ball while he is in the air but also when the ball is within the court. This enables the server to hit the ball downwards into the court. Because the ball is 5–10ft (1.5–3m) in court by the time the recovering team can play the ball, the power of the return is greatly reduced. At the point of contact the server is in the air at full stretch. The ball should be struck slightly above centre in order to bring it down within the opponent's court.

It must be said that the jump smash service is the most erratic of all the different types of service as the ball can easily hit the

Your feet should again be shoulder-width apart. Throw the ball up as before but this time bend your knees more than for the tennis serve. Take your hitting arm back so that it is straight and pointing to the ground behind you. The other arm should be straight and pointing towards the ball. At this point your body weight should be on your back foot. The hitting action starts with a swivelling of the hips which turns the body towards the ball and brings the hitting arm upwards (it should still be straight). As the arm comes upwards the weight should be transferred to the front foot. At the point of contact your body should be upright and at full stretch.

The ball should be struck in the centre and with a slightly cupped hand. Once more, don't forget to follow-through, and get yourself into the game as quickly as you can.

Psychologically the service can place your team in an advantageous position. Good serving will inspire confidence amonst your team-mates. But bad serving will have the completely opposite effect. A faulty serve automatically gives the ball to the opposing team. Nobody likes giving anything away that easily, so make sure your serving is good and accurate. If it isn't, then practise it. You don't need anybody to practise serving with you. All you need to do is to go on a court, pick out various points and try to serve to them. Why not cut out four cardboard markers and place them at different points around the opposing court and try to serve to them . . . do not give up until you have hit each marker at least once. When you have done that, do the same again, but keep going until you have hit each one twice . . . and so on. It is practise, with an incentive. PRACTISE THE SERVES YOU ARE GOOD AT . . . PRACTISE THE ONES YOU ARE NOT SO GOOD AT EVEN MORE.

net or land beyond the base line. But when it is hit correctly it is dynamic and a potential point winner against all but the best teams.

The **windmill** serve is another overhead service but is made with the body at 90° to the net as opposed to facing it in the tennis serve.

If your team is not serving then the first task is to retrieve the ball and make a pass to the setter. So we will now go on to look at passing.

# VOLLEYBALL

# TECHNIQUE

The windmill serve (also known as 'the hook' serve). You can see why it is called the 'windmill' if you look at (c). Like the tennis serve, it is important to keep your eye on the ball but it is a serve rarely used today.

# VOLLEYBALL

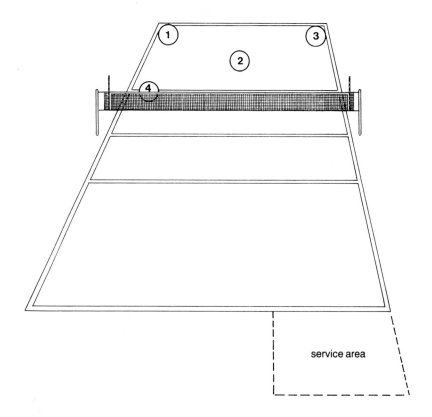

service area

*To practise your serve for accuracy, place four mats or chairs in the opposing court and try to serve to them. Try hitting the target with all three services: underhand, tennis and windmill.*

# *PASSING*

Passing can be made with either the **dig** or the **volley**.

The dig is normally used when (a) receiving the ball from the service, or (b) to play a ball that is too low to volley. The volley is played when the ball is above the head.

## The dig

The two hands are closed and kept together, and contact with the ball is with the forearms which are turned facing upwards. Do not swing your arms at the ball and keep your shoulders in a 'shrugged' position. While the dig is a passing movement, its prime function is to absorb the ball. Bend your knees before receiving the ball, but straighten them as you receive the ball on the arms. The straightening movement of the legs will effect the pass.

You must move to the ball and try and contact it at, or below, waist-level.

It is important that you keep your arms together and straight. You should imagine the area of the arm the ball hits as a 'floor' on which the ball is about to bounce.

To practise the dig, ideally you need a team-mate to work with. You can then set up an excellent practise programme to strengthen your technique as follows:

*The dig. How to hold the hands.*

*Note how the shoulders are positioned prior to making the dig. This is because the straightening of the legs does all the work.*

# VOLLEYBALL

(**a**) throw an easy lob to your partner for him to dig-pass the ball back to you.

(**b**) throw the ball, gently at first, towards his feet so he has to get down low to make the dig. After a while, vary the pace of the ball so he gets used to meeting fast balls as well.

(**c**) throw the ball 1m (3ft) in front of your partner so he has to move into the ball to make the dig. Again, after a while vary the distance he has to run.

(**d**) start throwing the ball to the right and left of your partner to get him used to positioning himself correctly.

When he has got used to that, start throwing low balls towards his feet.

You thought you had the easy job of throwing the ball to your partner didn't you? Sorry, but when you have done all that, reverse the roles! To make it nice and fair, why don't you just practise making dig-passes to each other; that way you are both practising the dig at the same time.

You can practise the dig on your own, but you will need a wall. Throw the ball against the wall and make the dig-pass back to it. You could even mark a target on the wall and try and hit that with your pass. To get used to the feel of the ball on your arms, you can practise by simply hitting the ball up and trying to keep it in the air as in 'head-tennis'.

*Getting ready for the dig. Arms outstretched and together, knees bent.*

If you are practising with all your team-mates, one player should take it in turns to be put under pressure from the rest. They throw quick-fire balls at him and he has to make a succession of dig-passes.

After taking part in some or all of those training sessions you will soon discover that the secret of the dig is to get *behind* and *under* the ball. As a beginner you are well advised to be content with successfully making the dig, and playing the ball into the air, rather than trying to direct it for a pass. This will come with experience.

## The volley

The volley is the most common way of playing the ball. The ball is always played in the air, and more often than not it is above head-height, so it is essential to be able to play the volley.

The volley is used to pass the ball, set up a smash, or to play the ball over the net.

The legs should be flexed at the knees with your feet shoulder-width apart. Contact with the ball is just above the forehead and is made with the fingers of both hands cupped around the ball. The palms of the hands do not touch the ball, full contact is by thumb and first two fingers. The other two fingers of each hand do make contact with the ball, but not full contact. Make sure the thumbs and fingers are relaxed and not tense.

Before contact the arms should be bent with the elbow at shoulder-height. They should be straightened as contact is made with the ball.

Because the volley is the shot you will use more than any other during a game you are well advised to practise it at an early stage in your development. Practise now will pay dividends later.

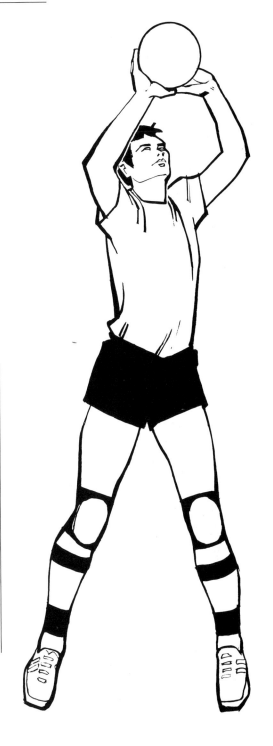

*The volley – the point of contact between hands and ball.*

As with the dig you can practise on your own, using a wall. You can throw the ball against it and volley back to it, better still to a target on the wall. You can also volley to yourself either standing in one position or by volleying in front of, behind, or to your side, and moving to meet the ball before making another volley. But for ideal practise sessions you should engage some or all of your team-mates.

However, if there are only two of you then try the following:

(**a**) stand about 1m (3ft) apart and volley to each other, standing stationary.

Concentrate on volleying the ball high more than anything. After a while, gradually move away from each other.
(**b**) to emphasize getting height on the ball, this time after playing each volley, sit down on the floor and get up again in time to play the next volley.

*The volley sequence. Keep those eyes on the ball.*

**Richard Dobell, England captain and setter, puts up an inviting set for a quick smash.**

*Player No. 8 is making the set, using the volley for No. 3 to smash. Note the position of No. 8's thumbs.*

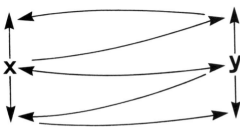

*A good volleying exercise for two players (X and Y). Pass and volley to each other moving to the left or right after each volley.*

(**c**) volley to each other as in (**a**) but start moving around, to your left and right; get your partner to do the same.

(**d**) find a target on a wall and make a volley to your partner who has to then volley to the target. Take this practise in turns.

If there are three or four of you practising together, then the following routines will come in useful:

(**a**) **Running relay** Two players form each team. The front players stand about 1–1½m (3–4ft) apart. A volleys to B and A

## Volley, setting and smashing exercises
*Running relay.*

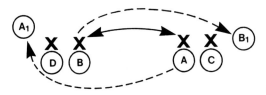

then runs to position A1. B then volleys to C who has now taken the place of A; B then moves to position B1 . . . and so on. Continue until each player has made five volleys. After a while, up this to 10, 15 and 20 volleys.

*Relay pass.*

(b) **Relay pass** Do as for the *running relay* but this time one player forms one team while the other is made up of two or three players. The three players take it in turn to run to the back of their 'queue' after making the volley. Again, continue until each player in the three-man team has made 5 passes, then gradually increase this to 10, 15 and 20.

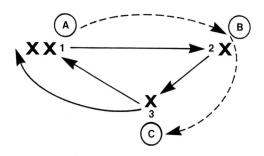

*Three man volley (1).*

(c) **Three-man volley (1)** Two players line up at position A, and one each at positions B and C. A, B and C should be about 2m (6ft) apart. The lead man at A volleys to B, who volleys to C. At the same time the first player at A runs round to replace C who takes up a position at the back of the 'queue' at A after volleying back to A . . . and so on. Continue as in (a) and (b) above.

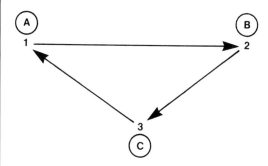

*Three man volley (2).*

(d) **Three-man volley (2)** A volleys to B making sure the ball lands about 1m (3ft) in front of B. He must then volley to C, A and C do not move, it is only the player at B who has to move into the ball. After five rounds, rotate one place clockwise so everybody has a turn at position B.

The best form of volleying exercise is with a smasher, and the following are actual match situations involving a setter and smasher.
(a) A throws the ball to B who stands close to the net, B volleys the ball for smasher (SM) to approach and smash over the net.
(b) as (a) except this time player B stands off-court and makes the volley at position B1 where the player A threw it to. Again, he must set the ball up for the smasher (SM).
(c) this time player B1 and B must make the successful volley for the smasher (SM) again.

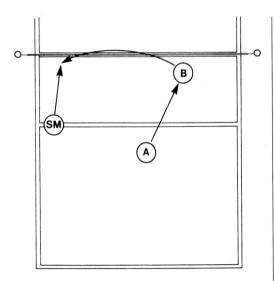

*Volley and smash (a).*

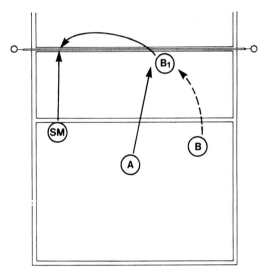

*Volley and smash (c).*

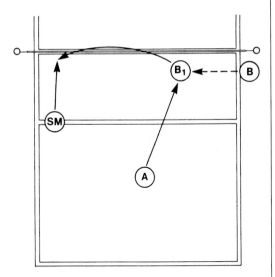

*Volley and smash (b).*

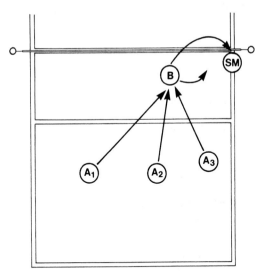

*Back reverse set and smash (a).*

As you gain more experience and confidence you can practise the **reverse volley**. Stand at position B, get player A to throw the ball to you from different points on the court, but each time you must make a reverse volley to the smasher (SM) who will remain in the same place.

A more difficult variation of this routine is to have the ball thrown about 1m (3ft) in front of you. That way you have to both move forward and make the reverse volley to the smasher. To make it even tougher,

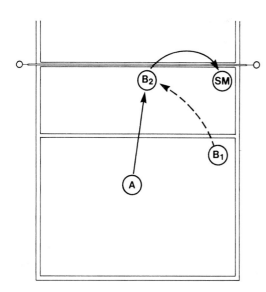

*Back reverse set and smash (b).*

practise the same routine with the volleyer on the attack line (B1). Get A to throw the ball to position B2. Player B has to then make the reverse volley to smasher (SM).

We cannot reiterate enough the importance of practising the volley. If you cannot volley, then you will never make a good volleyball player.

# *SETTING*

Setting is, as its name implies, the art of setting the ball up, by any player, for another player to make a smash (or spike). Setting is done close to the net and by means of a volley pass. The ball must be set up at a height above the net for the smasher to run onto in order to make a powerful smash.

On the previous pages we emphasized the importance of being able to make a volley pass with height. Now do you see why? So the smasher can get his shot in.

The exercises involving a smasher in the previous section are setting exercises and particular attention should be paid to them.

Setting is the second part of classic three-touch volleyball. But perhaps it is the most important. While it is the smash which earns the glory, and the points, it is no good having a good smasher in your team if he is not receiving good sets from his setters.

*Player No. 12 has set the ball for No. 9 who has gained maximum height to make the smash.*

*The reverse, or back, set made by No. 10 for No. 4 to smash.*

# TECHNIQUE

*Gaining maximum height to get above the
ball and smash it down is vital at the smash.*

Take advantage if one blocker is slow taking off and direct the ball over him.

*The smash. Note the arched back, the height gained and the follow through.*

# SMASHING

The smash is the most dynamic of all volleyball skills. It is the method of attacking the opposition and is the final move of classic three-touch volleyball. Technique for the smash, also known as the spike, is important.

The approach to the net should give you maximum height in your jump, so you don't want to start too close to the net. The approach starts 3m (10ft) from the net and is usually a three-step approach. The take-off is from both feet, rocking from heel to toe before take off. Step 1 is an adjusting step, to line up with the ball. Step 2 is to gain momentum for the jump, and Step 3 brings the back foot alongside the front foot. The last two strides should be made with the heel making contact with the ground first and with your trunk slightly leaning backwards.

Both arms swing forward and vigorously upwards to provide maximum lift and balance in preparation for the smash. You should jump as high as possible without travelling forward too much. The left arm is used for balance (assuming you are right-handed) and the hitting arm travels upwards, and bends at the elbow so it can travel through the greatest possible distance.

# VOLLEYBALL

*Not all smashes have to be powerful. The dump over the blockers can often be effective. This is known as the tactical ball.*

# TECHNIQUE

The ball is hit at the top of the reach and with the open hand. Make sure your wrist is relaxed, but not floppy, and that your fingers are firm but not stiff. The arm action should be fast and the smash aggressive. After all, you are trying to play a shot that your opponents cannot return.

After hitting the ball the arm should follow-through so the action is a full and vigorous one. Don't touch the net after completing the smash; it is a fault if you do. Also be careful not to step into your opponents' court.

The approach to the smash is important, thus enabling you to be in the correct position and have the best vertical take-off.

Ideally, you should be 3–4m (10–12ft) from the net when you make your approach. For a right-handed hitter, if making the smash from Position 4 you should stand just outside the court. If you are left-handed, then you stand just outside the court or on the side line when smashing from Position 2.

Timing is important. You don't want to arrive at the ball too early or too late. You should not start your approach until the setter has played his volley, and the ball is at its highest point. Timing a smash is often the hardest part of the game for a novice to grasp. If your team has a good coach he will help you in this respect. If you have trouble timing your approach ask him to put his hands on your shoulders and release them when he feels you should start your approach. Don't worry if you don't get it right the first time, keep practising and it will come good.

## The tactical ball

Leading smashers have the tactical ball amongst their repertoire. Sometimes also known as the **dump**, it is a delicately played smash as opposed to the conventional power-smash.

Some players seem to be reluctant to use the tactical ball but internationally it is a vital part of a smasher's armoury. The East Germans are the acknowledged masters of its use.

The approach, jump and preparatory movements are identical to the conventional full-blooded smash. And that is the key to it; your opponents must believe they are going to receive a full blooded smash.

However, as the hitting arm reaches its highest point, instead of making the smash the fingers of the hand are opened and they alone play the ball. The wrist and fingers of the smashing arm are the only parts which move. The wrist moves forwards (or to the right or left) and gives direction to the ball while the fingers provide the speed. There must be no movement of the arm from the shoulder or elbow once the ball has been contacted.

It is essential that the ball is not lifted but is placed to the side of, or over, the block and is kept as low as possible by flexing the wrist. If you pushed the ball high over the block it would give the back-line players plenty of time to reach it.

The most important factor when playing the tactical ball is placing it to a vulnerable part of the court. The placer has to be quick-thinking and spot a vulnerable part of the opposition's defence. The place where the ball is to be directed depends on the positioning of the opposing players.

The tactical ball is supposed to provide that element of surprise. Don't use it too often because your opponents will get used to it. Just as important, don't use it if your preparation is not right or you have not received a good set; the opposition will spot that a tactical ball is on its way and will move to deal with it.

It is a good tip to play a tactical ball early in the game. That way the opposition will know you have it as part of your repertoire and they won't know when to expect it.

Practising the tactical ball can be carried out in the same way as the setting and smashing exercises in the volleying section. But instead of smashing, place the ball over the net. Mark three or four numbered targets

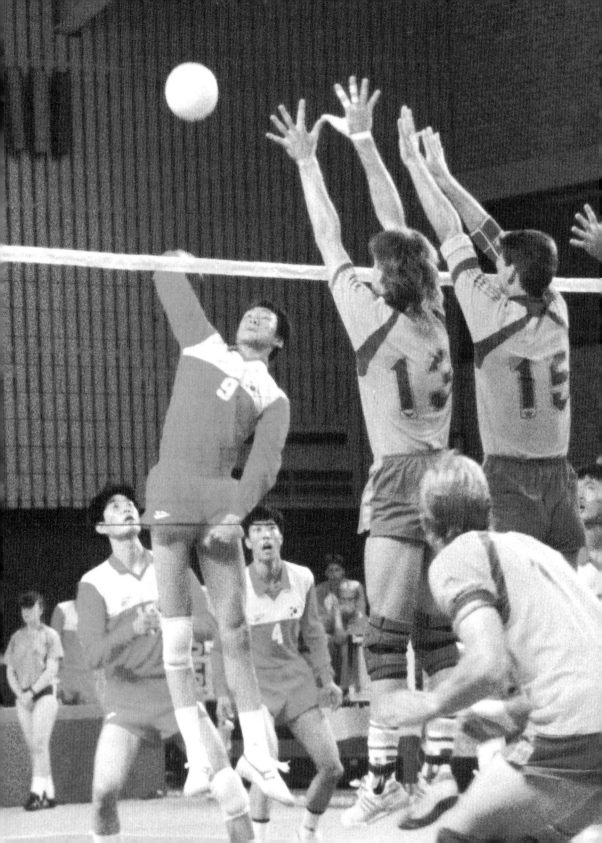

on the opposing court and get someone to shout a number out at random just as the set is being made. You have to then play the tactical ball to that numbered target.

The tactical ball is another form of attack, and a way past the opposing defence. Any skill which enables you to beat an opposing block is worth practising. So why not take a leaf out of the Continental teams' book and develop the tactical ball.

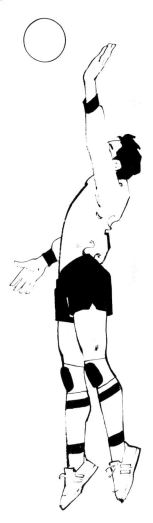

**The Swedish blockers present a united barrier to the Korean attack.**

# *BLOCKING*

So far we have looked only at the attacking aspect of volleyball, but there is a defensive side to the game – blocking.

Blocking is used to counter the smash or hopefully start an attacking move for your own team. It is carried out by any or all of the front-line players who jump and try to block a smash with their hands. If the ball remains in your half of the court after making a successful block, then the contact with the ball at the block does not count under the three-contact rules.

*Blockers can often turn the block into an attacking shot and possibly a winning point. One good blocker can also turn the block into an attacking shot.*

Good blocking can add up to five points to your score in every set. Bad blocking will give those five points to your opponents.

Before making a block, the front-line players should be aware of the position of the set in front of them and must know the

*Ready for the block. Knees bent and arms ready to be thrust straight up into the air.*

# TECHNIQUE

**Zhang Xiachua of China delivers a perfect reverse set for Sun Lijuan.**

*The block doesn't have to consist of three players. Two can be just as effective.*

opposing smasher's jumping ability and his approach and technique.

Once you have weighed all that up then you must decide where to position yourself. The next thing to consider is the jump. You want to jump as high as you can. Top male players should be able to reach a height at which their elbows are level with the top of the net. You can put your hands over the net into your opponents' court to make the block, but you must not touch the net.

As in the smash, timing is important. How embarrassing it would be if you jumped too early to make the block and had to stand at the net and watch the smash being made over your head.

After making the block, you must land, and quickly turn to face the play, either on your side, or your opponents' side of the net.

The four factors to remember when making a block are: (a) positioning, (b) timing, (c) jump, (d) aggression.

You should stand approximately a forearm's length from the net. Your hands should be held at shoulder-height, knees flexed slightly, and feet comfortably apart. You should be positioned opposite the ball and then jump as high as possible with arms stretched. As for knowing when to take-off, watch the smasher and take off a fraction after him.

The block should be made with open hands and fingers spread to cover as wide an area as possible and they should try and force the ball down into your opponents' court: this is an attacking block. You can do this against a smash that is made from not too great a height. However, if it is a very high smash then you are advised not to reach over the net but to make a defensive block instead. To do this you jump with your arms outstretched, but they remain on your own side of the net.

The number of players in a block depends on the situation at the time. All three front-line players may take part in the block for a high ball but it is more common to see just one or two men blocking.

That's it. We have taken you right from the basics, via the rules, and finally explained how to play volleyball. We said right at the start that it was an easy game to play, and it is. Furthermore, it is an enjoyable game to play. *Play the Game* has hopefully whetted your appetite for the game. The rest is now up to you. If you want to gain international honours you will not do so by reading books alone, you must go out and spend hours practising. But don't regard those hours as wasted, make them fun, enjoy them. That way you will get even more pleasure out of volleyball.

# USEFUL

# ADDRESSES

**International Volleyball Federation (FIVB)**
Avenue de la Gare 12
CH-1003 LAUSANNE
Switzerland

**European Volleyball Confederation (CEV)**
33 rue de Strasbourg
2561 Luxembourg

**British Volleyball Federation (BVF)**
c/o 27 South Road
West Bridgford
NOTTINGHAM
NG2 7AG
England

**English Volleyball Association (EVA)**
27 South Road
West Bridgford
NOTTINGHAM
NG2 7AG
England

**Scottish Volleyball Association (SVA)**
Castlecliffe
25 Johnston Terrace
EDINBURGH
Scotland

# VOLLEYBALL

**Irish Volleyball Association (VAI)**
20 Ardmore Crescent
Artane
DUBLIN 5
Republic of Ireland

**Welsh Volleyball Association (WVA)**
112 St Fagan Road
Fairwater
CARDIFF
South Glamorgan

**Northern Ireland Volleyball Association (NIVA)**
c/o House of Sport
Upper Malone Road
BELFAST
Northern Ireland

**Bengt Gustavsson of Sweden is one of the outstanding smashers in world volleyball. Here he hits over the Korean block.**

# RULES CLINIC

# INDEX

**The world's best all-round volleyball player Karch Kiraly
smashes past USSR's Valery Lossev.**

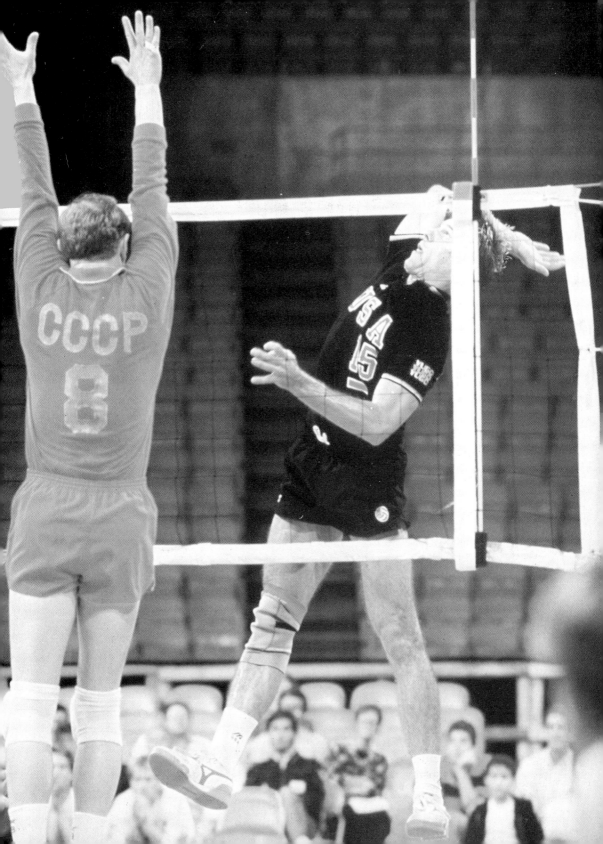

# INDEX